MOTHER TERESA

Her mission to serve God
by caring for the poor

by Charlotte Gray

MOREHOUSE PUBLISHING
HARRISBURG, PENNSYLVANIA

The highest award

The tiny nun, dressed in a thin white sari, stood on the speaker's platform before an audience of important, well-dressed, well-fed people. She had no notes. She spoke to the audience very simply, as if to friends. She told them of the world of poverty and suffering that lay beyond the walls of that building, of the streets of Calcutta, and of the misery that lies at the heart of some of the richest cities in the world.

It was December 1979 and Mother Teresa had come to Norway to receive the highest award there is – the Nobel Peace Prize. She was overjoyed, not for herself, but because the world was recognizing the poor she serves: "Personally I am unworthy. I accept it gratefully in the name of the poor." The money from the prize would go to feed the starving and to build homes for people who had none – the lost and lonely, the lepers, the outcasts. In fact, she received a little more than the $190,000 award. She also asked the committee to cancel the official banquet and let her have the extra money to feed those for whom a bowl of rice was a luxury. The price of that one banquet bought meals for fifteen thousand poor people.

A very ordinary sister

Mother Teresa was born into an Albanian family on the twenty-sixth of August 1910, in Skopje, Albania. She was the last of three children. Her family name was Bojaxhiu, and when she was just one day old, she was christened Agnes Gonxha, which means "flower bud."

It was a very happy family. Her father was full

"She embodies in herself compassion and love of humanity as few in history have done.... Her entire life has been a personification of service and compassion. These are the imperatives of human existence which are generally affirmed in words but denied in actions."

President N.S. Reddy, presenting Mother Teresa with the Star of India.

Opposite: Mother Teresa, with the Norwegian Prime Minister, shows her Nobel Peace Prize certificate to the world. She received it in Norway on December 11, 1979. At the time, the Washington Post *said, "Most of the recipients over the years have been politicians and diplomats.... Occasionally the Norwegian Nobel Committee uses the prize to remind the world there is more than one kind of peace, and that politics is not the only way to pursue it."*

This photo, taken in 1924, shows Agnes, who would one day become Mother Teresa, with her brother Lazar and sister Age. Agnes was fourteen and was quite fashionably dressed. The photo was taken not long before Lazar left for the military academy. When Agnes left to become a nun, she wouldn't see Lazar again for thirty years.

Above left: A rare early photo of Agnes, taken in September 1928 shortly before she left Albania to join the Loreto sisters. She would never see her mother or sister again.

Above: Agnes, aged ten, with some friends from Skopje. Agnes is on the extreme left of the picture. Agnes is wearing darker clothes than her friends because her father had died less than a year before, possibly murdered for his political activities.

of life and very much involved in politics; her mother, wise and strong, a little strict, but very kind.

It was also a religious family, devoutly Catholic, and Agnes' mother took the children with her to morning mass whenever possible. She taught them to say their prayers and to help her care for those less well off than themselves. Often, when their mother went to take food and money to the needy, little Agnes went with her. Every night the family recited the rosary together. "We were a very happy family," Mother Teresa often says.

Sadly, when Agnes was only nine, her father died. The family lost everything but its home. At first her mother was so grief-stricken that she left responsibility for everything to her eldest daughter, Age. But soon she regained her strength and set about building up a business, selling cloth and hand embroidery. From her mother's example, Agnes

Sister Teresa (left) and another novice at the Loreto convent in Darjeeling in 1929, when she was eighteen. It shows the two nuns in the dark, heavy dress of nuns from Europe. Twenty years later, Sister Teresa would choose to be part of the Indian nation and would wear a sari in the style of poor Indian peasants.

learned another important lesson: to greet adversity and poverty with an enterprising spirit.

In 1924 Agnes' brother, Lazar, left home to go to military school. The two sisters went to a local secondary school and both did very well. Agnes seemed to have a real gift for writing, and her brother thought that was where she would find a career. But by eighteen Agnes had made up her mind; she wanted above all else to become a missionary in India. In order to do this, she would have to become a nun. Her mother knew that if Agnes went so far away, she would probably never see her again, because in those days nuns did not come home for visits. But her mother understood Agnes' desire to serve the poor and did all she could to help her.

Agnes becomes a nun

The Yugoslav priests who worked in Bengal in India said that the Irish Order of the Sisters of Loreto were the nuns who served that area, so Agnes decided to ask them if she could join their order.

It was all very difficult. Agnes, along with another girl who wanted to join, had to go to Paris, the capital of France, to be interviewed by the Mother Superior. Agnes' mother and Age, in tears, waved goodbye as the train pulled out of Zagreb station, taking her away to a new life. How could they even suspect what the future held for her?

Just eighteen years old, Agnes aimed for nothing more than a useful, humble life as a Loreto nun.

The interview in Paris went well, and now the two girls were sent to Dublin in Ireland, to begin their training as nuns – their novitiate – and to learn English. They stayed for several weeks. It must have been a very bewildering time for them. People who knew them then only remember them as being very quiet and obedient and determined to master this new language.

It takes a long time to become a nun. The young women are taught what their life will be like and are given plenty of opportunity to make up their minds that this life is what they really, truly want. They do not make their final promises, their final vows, for many, many years.

The "Little Way"

At last, on the first of December 1928, when the six weeks were up, the two girls boarded a ship for the long voyage to India. They met three young Franciscan sisters on board and celebrated Christmas together. It was on January 6, 1929, that they arrived in Calcutta, the day the Christian Church celebrates the arrival of the Three Wise Men in Bethlehem with their presents for the baby Jesus.

Sister Teresa (top right) just after she had taken her final vows, in May 1937. She had just been appointed Principal of St. Mary's School at Entally, Calcutta. One of the other sisters described her as "delicate" – and there was no evident sign that eleven years later she would leave the convent to serve the "poorest of the poor." On rare occasions, Sister Teresa had to go to supervise the running of a local Bengali school. Unlike the other nuns, who were enclosed in the peaceful convent, Sister Teresa saw the bustle and poverty of the streets.

No one could have guessed what gifts Agnes was to bring to the city of Calcutta and to the world.

It was just over a year later, on May 23, 1929, that Agnes became a novice and changed her name to Teresa. This had been the name of a French Carmelite nun who had lived out her short life in a convent in Lisieux. She had taught that it is possible to serve God by doing the most ordinary, dull jobs as well as possible, cheerfully and gladly. She called it her "Little Way," and the new Sister Teresa thought it a very good way indeed. There was so much to learn, but Agnes was very, very happy, and on May 24, 1931, she took her first temporary vows of poverty, chastity and obedience.

She had only just begun her training and was sent immediately to Darjeeling, a town set in the foothills of the great Himalayas. She was to teach at the Loreto convent school there, but she also helped at the hospital. It was here that she first encountered suffering and poverty, the like of which she had never imagined possible. As she wrote later: "Many have come from a distance, walking for as much as three hours. What a state they are in! Their ears and feet are covered in sores. On their backs are lumps and lesions, among the numerous ulcers. Many remain at home because they are too debilitated by tropical fever to come."

Sister Teresa was happy at the hospital, and her work there was to stand her in good stead for what lay ahead.

When Sister Teresa's time in Darjeeling was over, she was sent to Calcutta. She left behind her the clear, sweet air of the mountains and the flowery meadows to live in the Loreto sisters' compound at Entally, a slum area on the eastern side of the city.

The sisters taught not only the children of rich parents, who boarded in the larger school, Loreto Entally, but also those from poorer families, who were taught in the Bengali language at St. Mary's, which stood in the same compound. It was here that Sister Teresa took up her job of teaching history and geography. She was a good teacher, bringing her subjects alive for her students. She was busy and happy, and it seemed her life would go on like this forever.

On May 14, 1937, Sister Teresa took her final lifetime vows. She was a professed nun at last and became Principal of St. Mary's School.

In those days, sisters kept very strictly within their convent walls, only leaving them if there was an emergency, like going to the hospital. Even then they were not allowed to travel on a bus, but had to be taken by car with another nun as companion. Sister Teresa lived in the quiet, calm atmosphere of the convent, and she enjoyed her work so much that she started teaching at St. Teresa's, a school outside the sisters' compound. The walk to and from the school gave her an opportunity to see for herself the real deprivation and poverty that existed in Calcutta and brought her face to face with the poorest of the poor. This was to prove to be very useful training for her in her future work in the slums of Calcutta.

But that was a long way ahead.

Violence and change

For nineteen years, as novice and then as professed sister, Sister Teresa lived the enclosed life of a Loreto nun. Beyond the walls, India changed – often with great violence, but within there was calm

The front gate of the Entally convent of the Sisters of Loreto. Sister Teresa spent over eleven peaceful years here, while World War II raged and India struggled for independence. The contrast of the peace and seclusion of the convent and the teeming slums outside the gates could hardly have been more striking.

and discipline and work and prayer.

Only a year after her arrival, Gandhi had led his peaceful march to stop the government from taxing salt — which even the poorest people needed. He and his followers were insulted, and many were badly injured, but the story of their courage went around the world.

In 1943, there was a famine in Bengal. Five million people died, and many fled to Calcutta. The streets were full of the starving and dying. Since the Japanese army occupied Burma, there were occasional bombing raids. The sisters evacuated their pupils. Loreto House became a transit camp for refugees, but Sister Teresa went on teaching in another of the mission's Calcutta schools and nursing the sick until normality returned.

In 1946, another disaster struck. Before the division of the subcontinent into Pakistan and India, there was great upheaval and violence. Muslims and Hindus fought and killed one another in the streets. More than four thousand people were killed during a five-day clash in August.

Though the riots were at their height, Sister

Teresa *had* to find food for her pupils, so she went out onto the streets. What she saw horrified her. There were bodies everywhere. The sisters had saved a Hindu and a Muslim who had taken refuge in their grounds that lay between Muslim and Hindu sections of the city, but they had had no idea of the extent of the nightmare that lay beyond the compound walls.

Stores had been set on fire with the owners inside, sewers were blocked with bodies that had been flung into them, and people were lying, bleeding to death, everywhere. Vultures circled above the stricken city. The air was full of screams and the sound of explosions.

A truckload of soldiers stopped Sister Teresa and told her to get back to the convent quickly. "But I *must* get food to my girls," she said. "I have three hundred students with nothing to eat."

The soldiers helped her – found her rice, took her back to the school and helped unload it.

Sister Teresa had shown what she was made of. The needs of others far outweighed any concern for herself.

The roofs of Motijhil (or "Pearl Lake"), the bustee, or slum, just beyond the peaceful gardens of the convent. Girls from Sister Teresa's school worked to relieve hardship in Motijhil, but because of the rules of the order, the nuns were not allowed outside the convent to join them. Because of her rare trips to supervise the local Bengali school, Sister Teresa was one of the few nuns who experienced the poverty.

Inspiration day

Only a month after what came to be known as "the Day of the Great Killing," Sister Teresa set off for Darjeeling by train. Every year the sisters would go up into the hills for a little while to think and pray in quietness: a little like recharging a battery.

On the way there, something happened to Sister Teresa. She did not see a vision – nothing so spectacular as that. She simply became utterly convinced that God wanted her to do something new, something she felt to be very, very important. It was September 10, 1946.

She referred to it as her "Call Within a Call," and her sisters celebrate this day every year as "Inspiration Day," because it was the very beginning of their order.

At first she said nothing to anyone, but she could not throw off the idea. So when she returned to Calcutta, she confided in some of the other nuns. She was absolutely certain that her life was to be completely changed. It was a startling thought. Here she was, nearly forty, a respected school principal, and now she believed God wanted her not only to give up being a principal, but to leave the school, to leave her order, to leave the protection of the convent walls. She believed he wanted her to go out onto the streets of Calcutta and live and work among the poorest of the poor, in the filthy slums beyond the convent walls.

To Sister Teresa, it was a direct command that she had to obey. And she had no idea at all how to go about it.

"She constantly found herself watching others go out to do the very work which she herself longed to do more than anything else. From her window in the convent she could see the misery of the Motijhil slums, stretching away beyond the trim lawns and tidy buildings of the Loreto property. It seemed that the only way to reach the poorest of the poor was to work outside the convent."

*David Porter,
from "Mother Teresa.
The Early Years."*

The long wait

Sister Teresa spoke to a priest she knew and trusted. He was stunned, but he said that when he had an opportunity, he would speak to the Archbishop.

It was not until the end of the year, when the Archbishop was visiting the convent, that the priest was able to talk it over with him. He listened carefully to Sister Teresa, but he did not like the notion of a lone nun wandering the streets of Calcutta. He decided nothing should be done for a year, to give Sister Teresa a chance to meditate and perhaps change her mind.

Sister Teresa accepted the ruling very quietly and went on with her work. She felt that if it really *was* a call from God, it would happen. A nun cannot just give up her vows and walk out of her convent, even if she believes she has an order direct from God himself. She has made very serious promises. The year 1947 was one of waiting.

No one else knew of her wishes or plans, but for health reasons she was sent to another convent for a while. She was put in charge of the kitchen as well as the grounds and went on teaching geography too. But it was not long before she returned to Entally to resolve a crisis at the school.

For a long while, it looked as though she would not be allowed to leave the order unless she gave up being a nun altogether, which was not what she wanted. But she said nothing. She just waited.

Leaving Loreto

At last, the decree arrived. It had been dated April 12, 1948, but it only arrived at the end of July. No wonder she had had to wait so long. The decree explained that she was to be released from the enclosure of the convent, but that she was still a nun and had to abide by her vows of chastity, poverty and obedience. It gave her a year to prove that her plan was a true call and workable. If at the end of that time nothing had come of her efforts, she would be welcomed back into her order with open arms.

When the priest, Father van Exem, told her that he had the reply, Sister Teresa turned pale.

He smiled and told her that she had exactly what she wanted.

"Can I go to the slums now?" she asked.

But, alas, it was not that simple. Everyone had to be informed.

Sister Teresa herself, although she longed to get on with her new work, found leaving very, very hard. Loreto had been her home, her family, for almost twenty years. As she said, "It meant everything to me."

Outside the walls

On August 8, Sister Teresa brought a sari, along with a small cross and a rosary, to the priest to be blessed. The sari was made of cheap white cotton, with lines of blue along its edge, the sort of sari worn by any poor Bengali woman.

This was to be her new habit, replacing the voluminous European dress she had worn for so long, with its skirt to the floor, its veil to the waist, its white coif around the head. This new dress was like the clothing of the poor and very practical to wear in the squalor of the alleyways that were to be her new home.

It was August 16, 1948, exactly two years after the day of "the Great Killing." It was an emotional farewell, with the schoolchildren singing Bengali songs and giving her presents. After spending some time praying, she slipped out of the convent gate in her thin white sari. No one saw her leave.

Sister Teresa believed she had been given a job by God himself, but she was a woman with a great deal of common sense. She knew that it was of no use at all to go out into the slums with nothing but a smile and a few comforting words.

She had arranged with the Medical Mission Sisters in Patna, 240 miles from Calcutta, to live with them for a few months, so that she could learn as much as possible about nursing the poor. The Holy Family Hospital was staffed by sisters who were doctors, some of them specializing in childbirth and in surgery, and by other sisters who were nurses, laboratory technicians and nutritionists.

They were very, very busy. They welcomed Sister Teresa, gave her a cubicle where she could sleep, and a place at the table. They included her in their day – which is exactly what she wanted. Whenever there was an emergency, they called the doctor – *and* Sister Teresa, who scurried across the lawn to stay with the patients while they were treated.

This courtyard in Motijhil, Calcutta, was where Mother Teresa opened her first school in December 1948. The school was her first project – started with no research, plans, premises or equipment. Forty years later, she would be launching new projects all over the world, with exactly the same lack of planning.

She coped with everything, watching, asking, learning. Nothing was too much for her, however tragic. She looked after cholera and smallpox patients, the poor, sick children abandoned by desperate parents, the injured and the dying.

The director taught her how to give injections and medicines and how to help deliver babies.

When there were weddings or feasts, when there was sadness or joy, she was there, getting to know the people, especially those who were ill. She was learning to understand them and to share their lives.

Advice from the sisters

The sisters were able to give Sister Teresa very good advice. In her enthusiasm she wanted to live on nothing but rice and salt, but they scolded her. How could she do a good day's work on a diet like that? She must eat sensibly, if simply, with plenty of protein and must not miss meals. She never forgot. When later young girls began to join her in her work, she made sure that they ate a proper breakfast of *chapattis* before they set off in the mornings.

The sisters had learned, too, that their white habits had to be changed and washed every day, sometimes twice a day. Sister Teresa remembered this, so all the sisters in her order would be issued with two saris, later with three. And they would all launder their clothes and have a thorough wash every evening when they got home from working in the slums.

In those days, little could be done to help some patients, but Sister Teresa gave them courage. One girl wanted so much to help Sister Teresa in her future work, but she was dying of tuberculosis, a disease of the lungs. So she did what she could, helping the other patients, talking with those who could not get out of bed. In a way she was Sister Teresa's very first follower.

Return to Calcutta

The time came to go back to Calcutta. Until she had decided what she wanted to do, Sister Teresa was to live with the Little Sisters of the Poor, an order that cares for destitute old people all around the world. When she left Patna, the sisters there gave her a present – a pair of sturdy sandals. Those sandals were to be repaired over and over and lasted a very long time. They were even shared by several of the young women who came to work with her!

It was December 1948, when Sister Teresa caught the train for the three-hundred-mile journey back to Calcutta, to begin her life with the poor. She was thirty-eight years old, her bare feet in the Patna sandals, a small black crucifix attached to the left shoulder of her sari with a safety pin, and only five rupees, that had been given to her by the Archbishop, in her bag.

For a few days she prepared her mind and heart for what lay ahead, and helped the nuns to take care of the old people who lived at St. Joseph's Home. Then, one morning, she went out into the slums of Calcutta, called *bustees*, to begin her new work. It was December 21, 1948.

The work begins

She had decided to begin in Motijhil, the *bustee* to which her students at Loreto used to go with Father Henry. It was about an hour's walk from St. Joseph's.

It was not long before Sister Teresa was visiting the slums regularly. To do her work properly, though, she needed some kind of shelter, but with only five rupees it was difficult to find a suitable place. After a lot of searching and praying she eventually found a small hut in Motijhil.

Sister Teresa had nothing, but she could make a start. She found a few poor children, a little open space and began a school. There were no chairs, no tables, no blackboard, no chalk – only children eager to learn and a sister eager to teach. She knew that reading and writing were the keys to a better life for them, so she got a man with a spade to knock the grass off the ground, took a stick and began to write the letters of the alphabet in the mud. The next day there were more children, and someone gave her an old table. Then someone

Today the Missionaries of Charity have more than 140 schools in India alone. In this picture of the first school yard in Motijhil, the sister at least has a blackboard and a table. Mother Teresa simply scratched letters in the sand.

Father Julien Henry was the local priest in Motijhil, and he knew Mother Teresa well when she was the Principal at Loreto convent. Father Henry had taken girls from her school to work among the people in the slums. His support was vital in the early years of the Missionaries of Charity because many of the more formal Catholic priests would not have agreed with the unconventional ideas of Mother Teresa. Father Henry shared Mother Teresa's belief in the need to work right among the most destitute Bengali people.

else gave a chair, and someone else a rickety old wooden chest.

At midday she needed somewhere quiet where she could eat the little packet of food she had brought with her and where she could find a drink of water. People were kind, but once she knocked at the door of a convent to ask if she could eat her meal there. They sent her round to the back, to eat under the stairs: they thought she was a beggar. She never told anyone the name of the convent. Not all the nuns and priests thought her wise. One said, long after, "We thought she was cracked!"

Mother Teresa herself, at the request of the Archbishop, has written down a little about those early days. "God wants me to be a lonely nun.... Today I learned a good lesson. When I was going and going till my legs and arms were paining, I was thinking how the poor have to suffer to get food and shelter."

She knew that the only way to understand the needs of the poor was to become poor, and the only way to gain their acceptance was to become one of them.

14 Creek Lane

Sister Teresa, who had lived all her life among people she loved and who loved her, now found herself alone and among strangers. She was very, very lonely, but she knew that this was the work she was meant to do.

Gradually, girls who had been her pupils at Loreto Entally heard about Sister Teresa's work and came to help her, as did the cook, Charur Ma. Charur Ma was later to live and work at Sister Teresa's children's home. As the numbers grew, the hut became more and more crowded. Mother Teresa knew she would have to find somewhere bigger so she asked the local priest, Father van Exem, if he could help.

The first big step forward came when a man called Michael Gomes, who lived with his family in Creek Lane, heard from Father van Exem that she needed somewhere to live and offered her the

use of the second floor of his house. Sister Teresa was very grateful. She moved in, and furnished it too – with a chair, a packing case for a desk and some extra wooden boxes to seat visitors.

People who had heard what she was doing sent small gifts of money to help buy things for her little school, but one of the greatest needs was for medicines to treat the sick people. Michael Gomes would go with her to all the pharmacies, asking the owners to donate the medicines that the poor people could not afford. One pharmacist in Calcutta said he couldn't help and carried on with his work. But Sister Teresa and Gomes sat there so quietly and patiently that he ended up feeling ashamed of himself and gave her a big box of useful things.

Early days

The Gomes family were good friends. Sister Teresa, as a nun, could not go out alone, so sometimes Mr. Gomes' eight-year-old daughter would go out with

From the very beginning of her work in Calcutta, Mother Teresa tried to help those who were dying, abandoned on the streets of Calcutta. Soon after she left the convent, she borrowed a wheelbarrow and wheeled a desperately sick woman from hospital to hospital, trying to find a bed for her. Eventually, the woman died on the street because no one would take her in. The task Mother Teresa was undertaking was seemingly endless, because three <u>million</u> people are homeless in Calcutta. But the important thing, in her view, is to begin and not to be daunted by the magnitude of any task.

her, feeling very proud to help. Sometimes his niece would go too.

One day they came across a hut that had been pulled down because the woman who lived there could not pay the eight rupees she owed the landlord. She had nowhere to go and stood bewildered, up to her knees in water and trying to shield a child in her arms from the pouring monsoon rain. He clung to her neck, burning with fever, as their few possessions drifted, sodden and ruined, in the water around them.

Sister Teresa sent her young companions back to their home and then went back to do what she could to help the poor mother. If she had not found them, the little child would have died there in the rain – and all for the sake of a few rupees.

There was so much misery in these alleyways, so much hunger and sickness and fear. Sister Teresa worked from morning till night, but there never seemed enough time to do all that had to be done. But she was sure this was only a beginning, and she was right.

After all, she had a proper address now. People could find her.

And her lonely days were nearly over.

The first helpers

On March 19, 1949, a young girl came to her door. Her name was Subashini Das. She had been one of Sister Teresa's pupils and was now in her last year at secondary school. She came from a very wealthy family but had decided to sacrifice her fine clothes and jewels so she could spend the rest of her life helping Sister Teresa in the Calcutta slums. She became Sister Agnes. As a mark of respect she took Sister Teresa's original name and was the first sister in what later became the Congregation of the Missionaries of Charity.

Only a few weeks later, another former student arrived. Her name was Magdalena. Her parents were bitterly disappointed that she was giving up the career they wanted for her, and it was two years before they understood and forgave her. She was to take the name of Sister Gertrude and to go on with her studies after all. Sister Teresa helped her with her mathematics so that her medical training could continue. Many years later, Sister Gertrude went out to Yemen and set up medical help for the poor people there. But when she knocked at the door of the house in Creek Lane, all that was far in the future.

By Easter, Sister Gertrude (Magdalena) and Sister Agnes (Subashini) were going about their work with Sister Teresa, using the buses and growing in confidence as they moved around the bustling, crowded city. Sister Teresa took good care of her young helpers, seeing that they ate properly, looking after them if they were ill, even if it meant staying up all night after a hard day in the bustees.

Soon a third young woman arrived, who became Sister Dorothy. Then a fourth, who became Sister Margaret Mary.

Five against poverty

Five women against all the suffering of a huge, sprawling, dangerous city. To anyone without Sister Teresa's complete faith, it must have seemed something very like madness. But she and the other sisters were committed, even though they could never have guessed just how much that first tiny community would grow.

Five women in blue-and-white saris, the first of all those who now carry Mother Teresa's example and love to the poor peoples of the world.

Sister Agnes, who is very shy and quiet, remembers those hard but happy days in Creek Lane well. They had very, very little money, though Sister Teresa told them they must never worry about that: help would come when it was needed.

One way Sister Teresa had of feeding the poor was to ask everyone in the parish not to throw away food, and she and the sisters went around all the houses collecting leftovers to give to the hungry. As Sister Agnes says, "How can you turn away someone who has not eaten for a day? You have to give something."

Sister Agnes, Mother Teresa's first recruit, joined in March 1949: "I was one of her students in Entally and have known her since I was nine years old." Small, quiet and self-effacing, Sister Agnes would stay with Mother Teresa as her closest aide and would handle much of the organization of the Missionaries of Charity in India.

The first novices to join Sister Teresa cared for abandoned and orphaned babies, and they found it difficult to cope with one or two extra babies arriving every day. But now the work has grown, and sixty to seventy abandoned children are rescued every day in Calcutta alone, and many, many more in the other houses around the world.

The wonderful Mr. Gomes

Michael Gomes and his family squashed up tighter and tighter to make room for the nuns. He never took money for rent, and he often gave them food and other useful bits and pieces.

He was very sensible too. Once, he saved Sister Teresa from making a bad mistake. The government offered to give her thirty-three rupees for every child in the Children's Home she had set up. She was delighted and agreed. Mr. Gomes said this was very unwise. She was puzzled, but six months later she met him in the street and said, "I have been singing on the tram coming back from government headquarters. I am so happy. You were quite right. They would have insisted I spend exactly thirty-three rupees on each child, but I can manage perfectly well on seventeen rupees a child. There are *so* many children. It would not be fair to give more to one than the other, and I can make any money I have go further if I have the freedom to spend it as it is needed."

Making and breaking rules

Long after those first days in Creek Lane, Mother Teresa, as she was by then, set up a school called Protima Sen. It was to help children who were beyond their parents' control or in trouble with the police, children who had drifted on to the streets and into thieving and worse. Mr. Gomes, who had become a teacher there, was proud of the way the children worked to make a better life for themselves, and he wanted to hire someone to teach them the classical Manipuri dancing. Sister Teresa thought this would be an extravagance and said no, but Mr. Gomes secretly set the dancer to work.

Later, Mother Teresa came to the school to see a show the children were putting on for her. She was amazed by their beautiful dancing. "It's wonderful," she said. "It is a sin not to develop talents like this!"

Mr. Gomes laughed and told her that it was *he* who had "sinned," for he had disobeyed her!

And then she laughed too, happy that she had been wrong and her friend right. As Mr. Gomes said, "She makes rules and she breaks rules. That is her strength."

Work and play

The sisters didn't have many possessions, but they managed to have a lot of fun. Mr. Gomes has said you could hear their laughter all over the house and from the top of the street. When they were not working or praying they would play hopscotch and tug-of-war.

Sister Teresa seemed to be everywhere.

When she was able to get hold of flour from the government food stores she would return, sitting in the back of the truck, on top of the sacks. If she hadn't, much of the flour would have been stolen.

Michael Gomes lent part of his house at Creek Lane to Mother Teresa and her first novices. Eventually there were nearly thirty of them living in a large upstairs room and doing their washing on the roof. Michael Gomes thought that to have Mother Teresa under his roof was a blessing. "We received. We did not give," he said.

It was not fair, she thought, to make the other sisters do the job of guarding the flour.

Mr. Gomes used to be amazed at her staying power. Sometimes she would go out at eight in the morning and not get home till four or five, and she would not even have had a drop of water. Even in her late seventies, she would be just the same, working twenty-one hours a day.

Sometimes she overdid things, and the sisters and the doctor would have to bully her into bed for a rest. But she was always back to work as soon as she could get to her feet. Once she fell ill, and a message came from a Hindu gentleman that touched her deeply. He told her he had been praying to the goddess Kali to make her well soon so that she could come back to her people, who needed her.

Growing and growing

The sisters were not yet recognized as a proper order by the Catholic Church and with a set Rule, but they lived as nuns and they were absolutely certain that one day they would be officially accepted. After all, it was less than a year since Sister Teresa had left Loreto.

Sister Teresa made sure that the work the sisters did in the streets did not interfere with their education. She drew up very careful schedules so that they had time for everything.

Some of the girls, of course, found the life too hard and left, but the few weeks they had spent with Sister Teresa were never wasted. They learned things that they never forgot. Sister Teresa knew that everyone has their own special job to do in life and that not every woman is meant to be a nun. The girls who left would find their vocations in other work.

The number of sisters grew. Mr. Gomes gave them a larger room, and then the loft. The sisters even had extra bathrooms, made of bricks and bamboo matting, built on the roof! But it was very crowded. It was good they had so few possessions!

The sari-clad girls went out into the very poorest areas, taking care of the children and of the people who were dying without any care in the alleyways

Opposite: Mother Teresa's religion is, for her, the central pillar of her life. "My life is devoted to Christ," she says. "It is for him that I breathe and see. I can't bear the pain when people call me a social worker. Had I been in social work, I would have left it long ago."

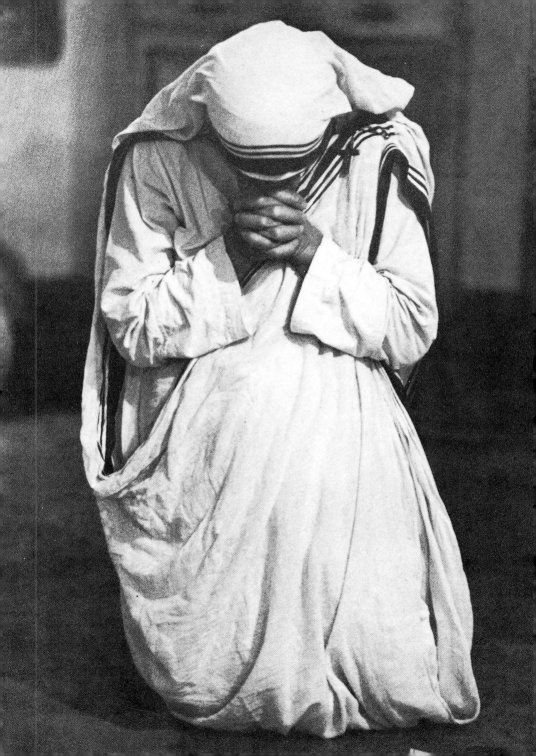

of Calcutta. Sister Teresa took an equal share in everything that had to be done – even cleaning the toilet. She would never ask anyone to do anything she would not do herself.

The Missionaries of Charity

When the trial year was up, the Archbishop gathered together all the information he could about Sister Teresa and her band of helpers. Some cross old priests simply did not understand what they were trying to do and thought they would all

By the end of 1950, Sister Teresa already had twelve helpers. Their numbers grew slowly but steadily. By the mid-1960s, when vocations to other orders were dropping by over 50%, the pace of recruitment to the Missionaries of Charity doubled and redoubled. By 1988, there would be over three thousand sisters and novices. And worldwide, there would be seventy thousand Co-Workers.

be better off safely behind convent walls. But everyone else could not praise them too highly. The sisters were brave and kind and cheerful, and they were doing work that could be done no other way. People were wondering how they ever managed without them.

Sister Teresa took Indian citizenship. Now she was truly one of that country's poor.

She wrote out very carefully the aims of her little group and the Rule they followed. To the usual vows of poverty, chastity and obedience she added "to give wholehearted and free service to the

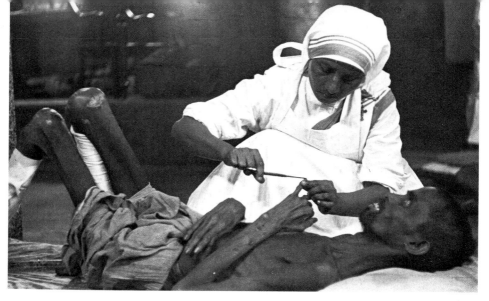

This nun is cutting a dying man's fingernails and cleaning his septic sores. The sisters have always deliberately chosen what most people regard as the worst jobs. For example, when civil war later struck in 1971 in nearby East Pakistan (now Bangladesh), over a million refugees flooded into India. Thousands of aid workers from all over the world flew into Calcutta to help. The Missionaries of Charity concentrated on the most basic jobs – the cleaning and burying of the dead – to avoid a cholera outbreak and so to enable others to run the feeding schemes.

poorest of the poor."

The Archbishop was very moved and impressed by what they had done in so short a time and by what they intended to do in the future. The constitution was accepted and, on October 7, 1950, the Missionaries of Charity order was recognized by the Catholic Church and approved by the Pope. The sisters promised that they would "seek out in towns and villages all over the world, even amid squalid surroundings, the poorest, the abandoned, the dying, the desperate, the lost, the outcasts, taking care of them, rendering help to them, visiting them assiduously, living Christ's love for them."

Sister Teresa becomes Mother Teresa

Sister Teresa, once teacher and headmistress of Loreto, was now Mother Teresa, founder of the Missionaries of Charity.

Even she could not have guessed the extent to which the promises in her mission's constitution were to be fulfilled. If you look at the back of this book, you will find a list of the dozens of countries where the Missionaries of Charity work. When Mother Teresa first stepped out of St. Joseph's into the streets, she believed she was embarking on something important, but she could not have known then, lonely and empty-handed as she was, how far and wide her message was to reach.

Her people were to be the people no one else valued or had time for, the expendable people, who just did not matter. To her, and to her sisters, every single person, however deformed, however dirty or diseased – the babies thrown away on rubbish heaps, the old left to die alone, the mentally ill, the outcasts of society – were all valuable, important, infinitely precious. It did not matter at all what their race was, or religion. In each of them, as she said, she "saw her God himself, in distressing disguise."

She did not just help them. She loved them. And always would.

The Missionaries of Charity take a vow of absolute poverty, and most of their possessions are held in common. No sister is allowed to receive personal mail or personal gifts, and she is not allowed to read books unless they are religious. Here a line of communally owned umbrellas wait for any sister going out into the heavy monsoon rains.

The Motherhouse from a Muslim

In the next two years, the number of sisters grew to twenty-eight. However much everyone squashed into corners, the house in Creek Lane just wasn't big enough. Father Henry and another priest cycled all over Calcutta, looking for somewhere large enough and cheap enough to hold the whole community and allow it to expand. Some of the houses more or less disintegrated as they looked over them, the floors collapsing under their feet.

With the division of India, a great many Muslims were leaving their homes, often with sadness, to go and live in Pakistan, the part of India set aside for them, for violence was still breaking out between the Muslims and the Hindus. One of these Muslims was an ex-magistrate, an old friend of Father van Exem. They were talking in front of his house when he suddenly asked the priest to wait for a moment and went into a nearby Mosque. After a while he came back and said "I got the house from God, I give it back to Him."

And so Mother Teresa's first proper house, the Motherhouse of her Order, the base from which all the hundreds of groups of sisters were to spread across the world, came from the generosity of a Muslim. As Mother Teresa knew, it is mankind, not God, who divides people up into boxes with different labels.

Waste not, want not

The Motherhouse at 54a Lower Circular Road, Calcutta, is a place of great peace and serenity. It is like a quiet haven where the sisters can rest before setting out on the seas of the world's suffering. But even there Mother Teresa has been known to break her own rules! A starving man came hammering on the door. Firmly but quietly Mother Teresa told him to go next door to get something to eat. But still he hammered. Mother Teresa looked at him, went inside and came back with two plates of food, which she gave him, plates and all. I wonder what dinner the sisters who were out got when they came home? The starving man had had theirs – *and* their plates.

Time and again in the early days, Mother Teresa went hungry so that others could eat, or gave people her fare and walked home. From the very beginning, whenever a banquet was to be given for her, she would ask that it be cancelled and that the money it would have cost be given to the poor. On air trips she set the sisters an example by asking for a big doggy bag, so that all the unwanted food could be collected for the poor. It is very hard for any of the sisters to see food wasted, with the recollection of the starving. They never, never accept the offer of a meal or a drink, even knowing it will offend those people whose hospitality they have to refuse.

"We must never think any one of us is indispensable. God has ways and means. He may allow everything to go upside down in the hands of a very talented and capable sister. God sees only her love. She may exhaust herself, even kill herself with work, but unless her work is interwoven with love, it is useless."

Mother Teresa.

Shishu Bhavan

If the Motherhouse is a haven of tranquility, the sisters' work headquarters is not. Called Shishu Bhavan, it is very near Creek Lane, where everything began, and is a very busy place indeed.

You go in through a little side door. Just inside is a grotto, where the people needing help can sit in the shade until someone comes to see to them.

The sisters and their helpers cook the food in containers, battered but clean, in the nearby kitchen, or hand out medicines from the dispensary. The sisters treat everyone in need as if they are very special.

A special love

The most special of all, of course, are the children. Sometimes so many tiny babies have been brought in from the streets, where they have been found abandoned, that two or even three have to share a bed. Many are so small and weak and ill that, although the sisters try in every way possible to save them, they die. But as Mother Teresa herself said, at least for a few hours of their little lives, they would know love and gentleness.

However, many babies – some weighing less than two pounds when they are brought in – manage to pull through and grow up to live happy lives. Every one that does is a joy to the sisters who have saved it, and who watch it slowly gain weight and strength. Little children who were too feeble even to crawl find their feet and toddle about triumphantly.

The sisters started feeding small groups of starving people. The numbers grew rapidly, but so did the matching donations and food relief. Every day now, six thousand people are fed in the worst slum areas of the world.

The sisters do not just wash them, feed them, and tend to their injuries, but give them love and attention. They cuddle them and play with them and let them know they are wanted. Even those who are going to live are often still covered with sores or twisted by rickets, a condition caused by malnourishment. Many are treated for lice or for a sort of parasitic worm. Some are mentally retarded. All are loved and valued. All are special.

Stories of caring

Wonderfully, more and more children are adopted. The French, the sisters say, are especially good. They often adopt children who have very serious things wrong with them. The children go off to grow up in France with their new parents or to other countries around the world, or to families in India itself. Some are too disabled ever to be adopted, but the sisters care for them all their lives, and often find things for them to do that make life better for them.

One little boy had no one. His grandmother who had raised him knew she was dying, so she brought him to Shishu Bhavan. The sisters took him in and saw that he was educated. Even when he was tiny, whenever anyone asked what he wanted to be when he grew up, he said, "I am going to be Mother Teresa." He couldn't do that, but he did become a priest and now works to help people, just like Mother Teresa.

The sisters sponsor one or two children in big, poor families, seeing them through school so that they can eventually get jobs and help the others. Without the sisters' help these children would have no chance, brought up with no place to study, nowhere to play, a miserable, crowded room to sleep in and never enough to eat. Can you imagine living on only one meal a day? Or living under a piece of rag on the roadside, ignored by the busy passers-by?

Entire families may be abandoned or orphaned. One mother went without food for her children's sake. She became ill and died, and the eldest girl, who was only fourteen, had to care for everyone.

Mother Teresa cradles and protects a young child, one of so many who are helped. From now on in the story, nothing really changed and Mother Teresa's life became, in one way, uneventful. Each day, she and her sisters rose at 4:30 a.m., prayed, washed, loved, served, prayed, worked, loved, and served again. Day after day. Year after year. But in this very repetition, this steadfastness, this sticking to basics, lay her power and her strength. Over and over, she repeated the same fundamental message, "Serve Jesus in the distressing disguise of the poor." In different ways, she said many thousands of times, "Give until it hurts."

She was particularly worried about her smallest brother, who became so weak and unhappy that he never moved or made a sound – or even cried. A newspaper reporter, writing about Mother Teresa, mentioned the children in the press, telling how the sisters visited them and helped look after them in their little shanty. Seven thousand rupees were collected and given to Mother Teresa for them. She promptly banked five thousand rupees as a dowry for the girl, Rita, and set aside the rest for the other children. The reporter was rather indignant; it seemed a very strange way to use the money. But Mother Teresa was right. She was thinking like

an Indian. Without the dowry the girl could never find a husband or safety and security.

As it was, Rita was educated at one of the sisters' schools and married happily. The rest of the children found love and care with the sisters, and the little boy who could not cry was found well-to-do foster parents who loved him dearly.

One boy was found by Mother Teresa sitting under a tree. He had run away from a cruel uncle and aunt, who never gave him enough to eat and worked him too hard. He was living by his wits, begging and stealing. Mother Teresa brought him to Shishu Bhavan and sent him to school. He did well, but he was still very much alone. He told Mother Teresa that he would like to marry. She thought he was far too young, but he was so sad that she bought him a little plot of land on which to build a house. Two of the sisters went to his wedding, to act as the family he did not have.

Some people thought they could get cheap servants from the sisters, believing the poor would take *any* wage, however small, and do any work, however hard and unpleasant. Mother Teresa soon sent them packing saying, "If you cannot afford to pay a servant a decent wage and feed and house them properly, then you cannot afford a servant. If these are hard days for you, they are worse for the poor. Why should they suffer more?"

Sealdah Station

Two years after the establishment of the Motherhouse, the Missionaries of Charity had become a familiar sight in Calcutta.

The sisters went wherever suffering called them. One especially sad place was the Sealdah Station, the terminal of the Eastern Railway. There, ten thousand people cooked and ate and slept and died on the stone floors of the huge waiting rooms and open areas, as the trains came in and out and the passengers picked their way around them. Every day, government officials came, choosing fatherless families to be housed in camps in the country. But every day more people arrived to replace those who had left. The sisters did all they could, but it was

Opposite: The sisters started work among the homeless at Sealdah Station. For decades, an average of four thousand destitute people have flooded into Calcutta each day. Whenever there is a drought, thousands more refugees arrive. The big rail terminals have always served as refuges. Nowadays this operation is run by the Missionary Brothers of Charity.

a desperate situation.

They handed out a bulgar wheat and soya mixture, supplied by the relief agencies, to any woman who had a stove. It did not taste as good as rice, but it was very nourishing, and the people became used to it. At least it kept them alive.

For those who had nothing, the sisters cooked the mixture in big vats and doled it out in ladles. The government did all it could to help, but it was never enough. There were just too many hungry mouths. Those people who could went into the city, trying to earn even a few rupees doing odd jobs.

The only water available came from the station washrooms. There was a stench of disease and dirt, of rotting food saved for the next meal – and everywhere the smoke from the little cooking fires.

The sisters had so many people to care for in Calcutta they could only come to Sealdah a few days a week, but they always searched the crowds for people seriously in need of help, taking little children who were very ill to Shishu Bhavan.

Life on the streets

At that time there were between six and eight million people living in Calcutta, and of those, two-hundred thousand had no home but the streets.

Mother Teresa once found a woman half eaten by rats and ants, lying in the gutter. She was so weak she could do nothing to help herself. Mother Teresa gathered her up in her arms and carried her to the nearest hospital, but they refused to admit her. The woman had no money at all, and she was dying, and the people there thought they could bully the tiny nun into taking her away. They had picked the wrong nun. Nothing could move Mother Teresa. She could be as brave as a tiger, and she stood her ground. The hospital let the poor, dying woman have a bed. Years later when people said, "What is the use of of even *trying* to deal with all this misery?" Mother Teresa would say, "If I had not picked up that very first woman, none of the thousands, millions, of people who followed would have been helped. There always has to be a very first step on any journey."

Even the Indian Government doesn't know how many people live in Calcutta. Officially, there were nine million in 1980, today there are probably nearer twenty million. No matter how many people the sisters are able to help, there are always others, like this man, who died alone on the streets.

It did not always turn out so well. Sometimes Mother Teresa was forced to take her pitiful burden from hospital to hospital by taxi, turned away from every door, and often the taxi driver refused to take her further, leaving patient and nun stranded. The hospitals had their reasons. Often they themselves had not a square foot of space left, especially for someone infectious and in need of long-term care.

When no other transport could be found, Mother Teresa would borrow a workman's wheelbarrow and push her suffering patient on to the door of the next hospital. What else could she do? She could not throw them back where she had found them. "We cannot let a child of God die like an animal in the gutter," she said.

Once she rented a room and took a man there that no one would accept. And then another. It did not matter how dirty and diseased they were, how repulsive to look at and touch. Even if there was nothing she could do to save them, she wanted them to die with dignity, surrounded by the love and kindness they had perhaps never known.

This picture shows why no one knows how many people there are in Calcutta. These are twelve "homes" for the people who wash, eat, live and die on the roadsides of Calcutta.

There *had* to be a solution. She went to the authorities and begged them to find her somewhere, anywhere, to take these poor people. She said that pet dogs would not be left to die as these human beings were. The Health Official of Calcutta looked at her. Here was a woman who had given up everything – money, freedom, even her nationality, to serve the poor of his country. He must find her something.

Nirmal Hriday

He asked her to go and look at a building that had once been the pilgrims' hostel of the Temple of Kali, the Hindu Goddess after which Calcutta is named. It was empty and filthy, but it had two sleeping wards, electricity, gas and a large enclosed courtyard. Mother Teresa's heart lifted. Immediately a group of sisters began to clean it from top to bottom – as only nuns can clean – and to get everything ready. They worked with such enthusiasm that only a week later, the first patients were able to move into Mother Teresa's new hospice for the dying, called Nirmal Hriday, "Place of the Pure Hearts."

The long hall was divided down the middle by a passageway, and on either side were raised cement platforms, with mattresses laid along them, side by side. Young, old, Hindus, Christians, Muslims, Anglo-Indians – dying people from every part of India – all found a home there, and peace and loving kindness. And the sisters always see to it that anyone who dies in Nirmal Hriday is buried according to the rituals of their own faith.

Mother Teresa accepted this building, now called the Nirmal Hriday, in 1952. The people who come here often have absolutely no hope; the hospitals in Calcutta are swamped with urgent cases and have to restrict the beds to people with a good chance of recovery.

The Hindus object

As the hospice was so near the Temple of Kali, many Hindus objected very strongly to Mother Teresa's presence, as she was a Christian. The sisters were even threatened with violence. Mother Teresa said, smiling, "We will only go to God sooner."

Then one of the priests from the Kali Temple became very ill with tuberculosis, so ill that no hospital would take him in. But Mother Teresa did.

In the hospice he was treated with the gentleness and love shown to all who lie in the rows of pallet beds. By the time he died, his fellow priests had found a new respect for the sisters, who gave all and asked for nothing.

That was not the end of the troubles. Some other Hindu priests thought Mother Teresa would try to convert her patients to her religion and wanted the Police Commissioner to evict her and her sisters. Their leader strode into the hospice, determined to force Mother Teresa out, but after a while he went back to his friends. He had seen the sisters washing and feeding those helpless people, seen them gently dressing their terrible wounds.

He told the protesters that he would gladly throw out Mother Teresa and the sisters – if they would persuade *their* mothers and sisters and daughters to take on the job instead, working day and night in poverty, as the sisters did. The group went away and never came back.

Charubala

You would think it would be a dreadful place, this house for the dying. But it is not. The sisters joke and laugh with those who can tease back. They coax the feeble to eat, hold the hands of those who are afraid or in pain. Whatever they have to do, they do as if it were the best and happiest work in the world.

Some of the patients had never known love or kindness. To them the bare rooms of Nirmal Hriday were as perfect as a luxury hotel. One lady, named Charubala, had lived all her life as a near-slave. When she was old and paralysed, she had been thrown out into the street, where Mother Teresa found her.

The sisters washed her gently, combed her hair, dressed her in clean clothes, laughed with her and listened to her songs. She could still use her hands, so she helped to feed Mary, the woman next to her who was too weak to feed herself. Charubala had a special friend who often came to see her, a Jesuit

"Today, talking about the poor is in fashion. Knowing, loving and serving the poor is quite a different matter."

Mother Teresa.

priest who loved music and for whom she made up songs. He learned to sing one of them.

"The evening has come. Those who come after me have gone before me. I, who came here months before them, must stay after they have gone. God, when will you take me away? Those who came after me have gone before me."

A special kind of hospital

The sisters knew this was not a hospital where people would mostly get well and go away. But there was little sadness. One visitor asked what she might bring that would please them. "Oh, grapes," said the sister, "I don't know why – perhaps it is because they are such a great luxury. And some ask for fresh oranges or sweets. A lot of the men like a cigarette. We try to give them any little thing that might bring them comfort."

These people who are brought in as living skeletons, their wounds alive with maggots, their filthy rags running with lice, are welcomed without even a flicker of disgust. Only gentleness and concern.

One man, ill as he was, was embarrassed by their kindness. "My wounds smell so horrible, Sister" he said. "How can you bear to come near me?"

The sister did not lie to him. "Of *course* they smell," she said, "but how can I worry about that, when I know the pain you must be suffering? It doesn't matter a bit about the smell."

Ordinary people turn up at Nirmal Hriday sometimes, to help the sisters for a while. They help with the feeding and washing, with cleaning the floors, with the cooking. They feel it a very great privilege, as though they are being allowed to do something very special. Whatever they do in their lives later on, they never forget the time working beside the sisters.

Becoming a Sister of Charity

Young women must have a deep desire to work with Mother Teresa. It takes nearly nine years to become a fully-professed Sister of Charity. Most candidates start as a "come-and-see," as Mother

"In these twenty years of work amongst the people, I have come more and more to realize that it is being unwanted that is the worst disease that any human being can ever experience. Nowadays we have found medicine for leprosy and lepers can be cured…. For all kinds of diseases there are medicines and cures. But for being unwanted, except there are willing hands to serve and there's a loving heart to love, I don't think this terrible disease can ever be cured."
Mother Teresa.

Opposite: Mother Teresa started her work with the dying by picking up one person. Then another and another. The sisters now run eighty hospices and care for over thirteen thousand dying people a year. To the sisters the important thing is that each person dies with the feeling of being loved.

The sisters start each day by praying together and return every lunchtime and night to eat, pray and sleep. There is much laughter in the houses and the sisters follow Mother Teresa's motto: "Together." This sense of sharing, of working and living together, helps to give the sisters the strength to do the work they do. It is physically heavy and very harrowing because of the suffering they encounter. Yet the sisters have a continual – and very obvious – aura of peace and happiness.

Teresa named them. At first, the young women work as assistants in the Shishu Bhavan and at Nirmal Hriday, washing and feeding the people, nursing the dying and cleaning up those brought off the streets. They also help feed the thousands that the Missionaries of Charity give a meal to every day across the world.

If, after a year, the girls still want to serve the poor and are still considered suitable candidates, they become novices and start their formal training. They choose their religious names and study the scriptures, theology, church history and the constitutions of the Society in great depth. They also learn to speak English, if they don't already know it.

They continue their service to the poorest of the

poor. In Calcutta, the novices run Nirmal Hriday and the other clinics and stations on Thursdays, replacing the professed sisters who return to the Motherhouse for a day of prayer and contemplation. Novices wear white saris, but without the three blue stripes of the professed sisters. After two years, they take their first vows, and then they receive their saris with the three blue stripes. They renew their vows at the end of the fourth and fifth years.

In the sixth year, the new sisters go to either Calcutta or Rome for a year spent in intense spiritual preparation for the life of sacrifice and hard work that lies ahead. Then they make their final vows and commit themselves for life to the Missionaries of Charity.

All her worldly possessions

Every sister is allowed to have three saris – one to wear, one to wash and one to mend – a pair of sandals, two sets of underclothes, a rosary and a small crucifix that is worn pinned on the left shoulder. Their underclothes are often made from old flour sacks that have to be washed about ten times before they are soft enough to wear.

Each sister also has a metal spoon and rimmed plate, a canvas bag (made by children in the bustees from ex-army cloth), and a prayer book. In colder countries, they usually have a cardigan. Coats and umbrellas are also available, but do not belong to any one particular sister. The sisters never wear socks or stockings, even in the snow.

Life at the Motherhouse

Imagine that you are in the Motherhouse in Calcutta. It is very, very early in the morning – twenty minutes to five. A bell rings. Out of the darkness comes the slap, slap of sandals on the bare floor. A quiet voice calls, "Let us bless the Lord," and the sleepy response comes from the waking sisters in the dormitory, "Thanks be to God."

The sisters go down to the bare quietness of the chapel. Outside the chapel is a blackboard that tells

"Her and the Sisters' and Brothers' identification with the poor among whom they live is no mere figure of speech. They eat the same food, wear the same clothes, possess as little, are not permitted to have a fan or any of the other mitigations of life in Bengal's sweltering heat. Even at their prayers, the clamour and discordancies of the street outside intrude, lest they should forget for a single second why they are there and where they belong."
Malcolm Muggeridge, from "Something Beautiful for God."

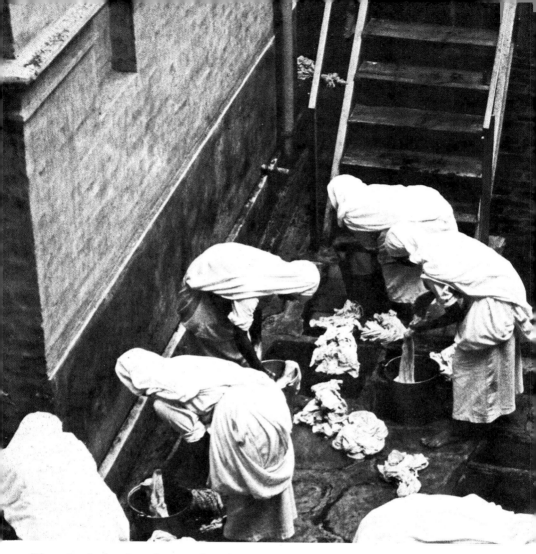

Thursday is the day when the Calcutta novices go out to run the clinics and schools so that the sisters can stay home to study, mend their saris and clean the convent. The sisters use tin buckets to wash their clothes, and all offers of washing machines have been cheerfully refused.

the sisters which saint is commemorated that day, the hymn to be sung, and lists people all over the world who have asked for prayers from the sisters.

Inside the chapel, the crucifix on the altar is surmounted with the words that are written in every chapel of the Missionaries of Charity all over the world, "I thirst." It is there to remind them of Christ's words, "A drink of water given to a beggar with compassion and love is a drink given to God himself." They pray for half an hour, kneeling on the floor. There are no seats.

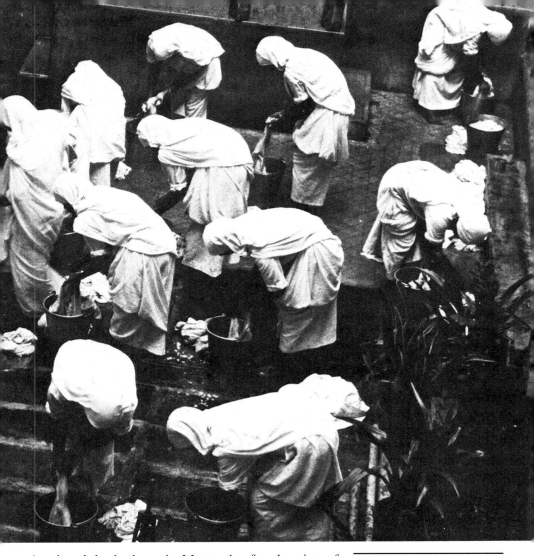

At six o'clock there is Mass, the focal point of their day. After Mass there is a breakfast of tea and *chapattis*. Then comes the cheerful sound of the sisters gathering up their supplies for the day, and setting out to different parts of the city — on foot, if at all possible, or by van or bus — a flurry of white saris in the busy streets.

The sisters always go in twos in the streets and they say words of the Rosary as they go. They often use the Rosary as a measure of distance, saying, "It's a three-Rosary walk." They carry what they

"I am sleeping on the table tonight," said an Italian sister laughing. "We change every month, and last month I was in bed but we have so many sisters living here that we have to sleep in the refectory, on the tables, on the benches and on the floor. I sleep very well."

In later years, Mother Teresa had to start using a telephone. She could no longer visit every house every two years. It seems to have made little difference to the smooth running of the houses, partly because, right from the start, she was single-minded – and she communicated this to the sisters. She defined the Missionaries of Charity's goals so well that the overseas sisters don't need to refer back to her on every decision.

"The rich, when they come to her, are liable to leave a little less rich, which she considers is conferring a great favour on them. On the other hand, she has never accepted any government grants in connection with her medical and social work. This, she says, with another of her quizzical smiles, would involve keeping accounts. I quite see her point. The administration of her whole organization is undertaken by two nuns with one rickety typewriter between them."

*Malcolm Muggeridge,
from "Something Beautiful
for God."*

need in their canvas bags; these always contain a bottle of water so that they do not need to ask for anything from the people they serve. They never accept food or drink from anybody.

A little after midday, the sisters return to the Motherhouse for a meal. The dishes are cleaned and yesterday's saris are washed in buckets in the courtyard and hung out on the roof to dry. Then a silence falls on the house. The sisters are all asleep.

Half an hour later, they wake up for prayers and the return to work. By two o'clock they are all out on the streets again, off to Nirmal Hriday or a school or a clinic or to work at the Shishu Bhavan. Somehow they seem to pack two days' work into one.

At six o'clock they come home. There is a short time in the chapel, then supper, reading and the chatter of voices sharing the excitement and trouble and oddities of the day.

Mother Teresa established a rule that, unless circumstances are exceptional, sisters do not stay away from the community overnight. So the sisters take turns staying overnight at Shishu Bhavan. Since extra workers have always been needed at Nirmal Hriday to lift patients and do the other heavy work, they run it at night. From the start, Mother Teresa knew it would be easy to lose the sense of community that binds an order together and tried to prevent this from happening. Her message, "Everything together," has become the sisters' slogan.

At the very end of the day, the sisters return to the chapel for night prayers. By ten they are in bed and fast asleep.

Not Mother Teresa of course. A writer once asked her how she managed to stay up into the early hours, writing letters, planning, deciding. She smiled. "I sleep fast," she said.

Gifts of love

Mother Teresa never worried that the money to do her work would not come. She was sure that it would. From governments, from the rich, and from the poor of countries in which poverty is not nearly as desperate as it is in Calcutta. For her, every opportunity to help the poor in any way was another chance to do something for God.

Small gifts, great gifts, money pushed into her hands on buses, trains, in the streets.

In 1964, the Pope visited India, and when he left he gave the beautiful car that had been presented to him for his journey to Mother Teresa. Now, no one could imagine Mother Teresa bowling around India in a white Rolls Royce! She could have simply sold it, but she was too smart for that. She auctioned it and turned the car into more help for her poor. In 1973 she was given a huge building that had been built as a chemical laboratory. She called it Prem Daan, which means "Gift of Love." There the very sick and demented people are cared for.

Just outside the gates is a little rehabilitation workshop. To this place the poor of Calcutta bring the empty green coconut shells that litter the city's streets. At Prem Daan they can be transformed into mats, rope, and bags; rubbish provides work

"She was outrageously brilliant. She made them [the journalists] laugh and she defined the terms of the questions they could ask her. She understood that the moral ground she occupied gave her the right to march up to airlines and ask for a free ticket to Washington, and once she arrived, to ask to see the President of the United States knowing he dare not refuse her."

*Bob Geldof,
from his autobiography,
"Is That It?"*

Mother Teresa's fame gradually spread, and ceremonies like the one above, to read a prayer of peace in London, or to receive dignitaries, like Prince Charles, happened more and more often. Among other awards, she received fourteen honorary degrees, the John F. Kennedy Award in 1972, and the Nobel Prize in 1979. But perhaps her most treasured awards were from India, symbols of recognition from her adopted country.

for nearly a hundred people.

Nothing is ever wasted. At Kidderpore there is employment only when the ships are in, but the sister in charge found a solution. She begged paper from anyone who could give it – from offices, churches, anywhere. The women made bags from it for the little stores and stalls of the city. Others do needlework and crochet. Families are able to live on the money made this way, and the women are busy talking and singing as they work.

Brothers of Charity

In 1963 Mother Teresa welcomed the first brothers, coming, like the sisters, from all over the world to give up all they had to work for the poor. By 1976 there were 175 brothers, with ten houses in India and two in South Vietnam, working with the sick and dying, lepers, juvenile delinquents, drug addicts and mental patients.

One brother, Father Ferdinand, had worked in a coal mine for six years and was earning a lot of

Mother Teresa delivers a message to the 9th International Congress of the Family in Paris in September 1986. In one way, the world fame, the prizes, the honorary degrees and the photographic sessions were all interruptions to the basic work she really wanted to do.

"I felt I had no business sitting beside this tiny giant. But there was nothing other-worldly or divine about her. The way she spoke to the journalists showed her to be as deft a manipulator of media as any high-powered American PR expert.

Bob Geldof, from "Is That It?"

money. He heard about Mother Teresa and went to Calcutta to help for a little while. He meant to stay for a month, but Mother Teresa spoke to him, and he stayed to take his vows as a brother.

You would not believe them to be brothers or priests if you saw them. They wear old workmen's clothes and, with gentleness and kindness, they wash and feed the emaciated, suffering people that are brought in off the streets. Like the sisters, they deal cheerfully with things most people run from.

Further and further

The world began to discover Mother Teresa. Schools, hospitals, shelters and clinics were springing up all over India, and the blue-edged saris of the sisters seemed everywhere.

In recognition of her work, groups and governments gave her medals and awards, and in 1979 she was awarded the Nobel Peace Prize. She accepted them all gratefully, for she saw them as not given to her, but to the poor she served.

So much had been achieved in India. To anyone else the work there would have seemed enough for any one lifetime – but, then, not everyone is Mother Teresa. She was sure that she must look beyond the sub-continent, to the poor of the whole world. If God wanted it, then he could make it possible.

Poverty can come in many different forms. In some countries it was very like that in India. In others it was hidden.

In 1965 she opened a mission in Venezuela; in 1967, one in Ceylon. In 1968 she visited Rome.

How could she find neglected people in a city crammed with hospitals and clinics and shelters?

The Barrachi

She found the Barrachi, the shacks built on waste land on the outskirts of Rome. There the poor had established themselves, making real homes from almost nothing, even growing cheerful gardens. The sisters took a leaf out of their book. When they installed themselves in the Barrachi, they put up trellises around their convent which were soon

Mother Teresa with Brother Andrew, then General Servant of the Missionary Brothers of Charity. Founded in 1963, the Brothers were formalized in 1966 when Brother Andrew left the Jesuits to act as director to the group of men who were trying to follow Mother Teresa's example. In 1970 there were still only eighty-six brothers. In 1988 there were 380 brothers who ran ninety-one homes in thirty countries.

draped with vines and planted flowers in old oil cans. However, unlike the more ingenious poor people, they had themselves linked officially to the city's electricity system!

Near the convent was a building some English students had constructed for the whole community. It provided day care for local children, a quiet place to study, a meeting place. From it the sisters went out into the homes of the poor, ready to cook or clean or wash up, to chat for a while, to write letters, to hang new curtains. The lonely old people watched eagerly for their coming – even the ones who liked to growl about the wickedness of the Church! The sisters saw that they ate properly, watched their health, brought them news and little presents. Whatever anyone's problem, they were there to listen and help.

The lonely world

Loneliness met Mother Teresa wherever she went – a poverty worse than lack of food or warmth. She found it in London, in New York: people pushed aside by a wealthy society, living in cold, lonely rooms or in boxes in the street.

In America she came across the drug problem for the first time. She sent her sisters there – and to London.

And on and on – Peru, Belfast, Venezuela, New Guinea, Australia, France, Ethiopia, Spain, Chile, Panama, Kenya. Three hundred convents were opened. Everywhere where there was hunger or fear, homelessness, loneliness or despair.

And always, everywhere, she begged the better-off to look around them, to recognize need in their own cities, their own streets. Sometimes in their own families.

Despair does not live only in the alleyways of Calcutta. It can live next door.

The poorest of the poor

So many people. No matter how hard the sisters worked, no matter how many schools they set up, there were always those beyond their reach.

"Be kind to each other in your homes. Be kind to those who surround you. I prefer that you make mistakes in kindness rather than that you work miracles in unkindness. Often just for one word, one look, one quick action, and darkness fills the heart of the one we love."

Mother Teresa
to the Co-Workers.

"Someone will ask, 'What can I do to help?' Her response is always the same, a response that reveals the clarity of her vision.... 'Just begin, one, one, one,' she urges. 'Begin at home by saying something good to your child, to your husband or to your wife. Begin by helping someone in need in your community, at work or at school. Begin by making whatever you do something beautiful for God.'"

From an interview
with Mother Teresa,
from "Words To Love By."

Opposite: Leprosy victims who live at Titagarh and other leprosy settlements make paper bags and sandals that can then be sold, and weave sheets and saris for the sisters. Despite the fact that leprosy is now curable, there are still over fifteen million leprosy victims in the world, with four million in India alone.

Below: Mobile clinics allow the sisters to reach patients in many more areas. They are particularly useful in helping victims of leprosy. Today, spread across the world, there are 670 Missionaries of Charity mobile clinics that treat over six million people a year.

All over the world, the poorest of all are forced to live in areas where no one else will live. Often they are the forgotten people. Mother Teresa knew Calcutta, and she knew where they would be. The trouble was reaching them.

The head of a relief agency, who had himself chosen to live among the very poor, had saved $25,000, and he wanted Mother Teresa to have it. With it, and other donations, she made a van into a mobile clinic. Now she could reach out to the desperate, those who could not afford to travel even a little way for help.

Every day it went to a different district. One was Kidderpore, where there was a Muslim community. The ladies who came to the clinic and brought their children were very shy, and their religion prevented their being treated by anyone but women. They totally trusted Mother Teresa, so she made sure she was always in the van on the day it went to Kidderpore.

The dust from the nearby docks and smoke from the little cooking stoves affected the children's eyes so that without treatment they often went blind. The sisters were too late to help all of them, but many had their sight saved.

Living conditions meant that many children had lung and throat complaints, especially tuberculosis. Mother Teresa had them X-rayed at Shishu Bhavan and they, too, were given hope of a better life.

A new campaign

The children, the starving, the dying, and the homeless – who could be suffering more than those the Missionaries of Charity were already helping? Those who had to endure not only poverty and homelessness and hunger, but leprosy, the disease that makes men and women outcasts among outcasts.

Mother Teresa had agreed not to take victims of leprosy into Nirmal Hriday but they were hammering at the door of the Motherhouse, begging for help. She had learned so much from that first mobile clinic. Now she set out to help the leprosy communities in the same way.

By 1956 she had established eight leprosy treatment stations throughout the city, the sisters visiting them every week in their bright blue treatment van.

People afflicted with the disease tried to hide it, to keep it a secret. Men told Mother Teresa that they had to leave their homes when they found the symptoms on their bodies. If they had stayed, their sons could never have found jobs nor their daughters found husbands. The only way to help such people was to seek them out and persuade them to come for treatment. Once they saw that people who visited the clinics were getting better, more and more followed their example.

Mother Teresa takes over

The government had closed the leprosarium in Calcutta, despite Mother Teresa's pleas, and had built a fine new institution well outside the city. The trouble was, the poor were afraid to go there, far away from familiar begging areas and their families. Despite a new mobile van from which the sisters ran clinics, Mother Teresa was certain that thousands of people still weren't getting help.

She did all she could. She sent Sister Shanti, who was trained in medicine, to learn more about leprosy. The more people who could be made non-infectious, the less the disease would spread.

She set up a street school for the children of those with the disease, very much as she had that first school in Motijhil. Quietly the sisters who taught them watched for signs of leprosy and so were able to treat it in its earliest stages.

But there was still nowhere they could take people who needed close attention. They had to treat them near their windowless, miserable shacks – and leave them there.

"I have never met anyone less sentimental, less scatty, more down-to-earth. Thus, until she [Mother Teresa] can accommodate her lepers in proper settlements where they can live useful, productive lives together, they still go out to beg in the streets of Calcutta if they want to. 'It's interesting for them,' she explained to me. If she happens to see them when they have come back, she will ask them how they have done."

Malcolm Muggeridge,
from "Something Beautiful
for God."

Titagarh

The rail company allowed the sisters to set up a treatment clinic on unoccupied land they owned at Titagarh, just as long as they did not put up permanent buildings. All around the huts the trains rattled and shrieked. There were, sadly, sometimes deaths when the maimed people tried to cross the lines, but despite everything, it was a place of cheerfulness and hope.

By 1976, thousands of leprosy patients had been treated there. Only the very infectious and ill were admitted as indoor patients, but five thousand attended the outdoor clinic. Many were completely cured, and more would have been if only they had understood the need to keep up the long treatment. The sisters knew education about the disease was as important as the treatment itself.

Touch a leper

The people of Calcutta who had in the past ignored the problem of leprosy that lay all around them – probably from fear – saw what the sisters were doing and began to take action. They put up big posters saying "Touch a leper with your compassion" and collected a lot of money.

At last a site of thirty acres was found two hundred miles from Calcutta and given to Mother Teresa by the government. There a wonderful new community was to be built – Shanti Nagar, the "Town of Peace." The plan was that hundreds of families afflicted with leprosy could move there and live happy, useful lives in little houses of their own.

And so the work grows and grows and grows. Every day thousands of dying people are being cared for, thousands of the very poorest people in the world are being fed. And feeling human care. Mother Teresa said it all started when she picked up one dying woman. And her work has grown quietly, step by step since then.

One woman, One world

A woman walked quietly out of her convent gates in August 1948, with a year to show that what she believed to be a call from God was real. All she had was her fare to Patna. What could she do, this little, middle-aged nun, trained only as a teacher?

She could change the world.

"Asked about the future of the congregation after her death she said, 'Let me die first, then God will provide. He will find someone more helpless, more hopeless than I to do His work.'"

Mother Teresa to a Co-Worker.

The Missionaries of Charity worldwide

The Missionaries of Charity are a rapidly growing religious order. They have grown since 1949 until they now have well over three hundred houses throughout the world, more than half of them outside India. They keep in touch through a newspaper called Ek Dil, which means "one heart" in Hindi. Mother Teresa tried to visit all the houses every two years, but the sheer numbers make this almost impossible. She was given a free pass for the Indian rail system and on Air India to go anywhere in the world.

The sisters work with many different kinds of need, from raped and pregnant girls who have been rejected by their families to AIDS victims in New York. The order is soon to start work in the Soviet Union. Seventy thousand "Co-Workers," who are not nuns, now help.

"At Shishu Bhavan, fires are lit in the courtyard every night. The enormous cooking vessels bubble with curry, rice and dhal ... seven thousand people are fed every day from this one place.... This pattern is carried out in one way or another at all the homes throughout the world."

Daphne Rae,
from "Love Till It Hurts."

The Houses around the world
(B = Houses of Brothers)
(C = Contemplative Orders)

Near East
Israel (2)
Jordan (1)
Lebanon (1)
Syria (2)
Yemen Arab Republic (3)
Australasia
Australia (7)
Papua New Guinea (4)
Asia
Bangladesh (7, 1B)
Hong Kong (2, 1B)
Japan (2, 1B)

Korea, South (2, 6B)
Macao (1, 1B)
Nepal (1)
Pakistan (1)
Philippines (11, 2B)
Singapore (1, 1B)
Sri Lanka (1)
Taiwan (2, 1B)
North America
Canada (3)
USA (20, 7B, 4C)
South America
Argentina (2)
Bolivia (2, 1B)
Brazil (4, 1B)
Chile (2)
Colombia (4, 1B)

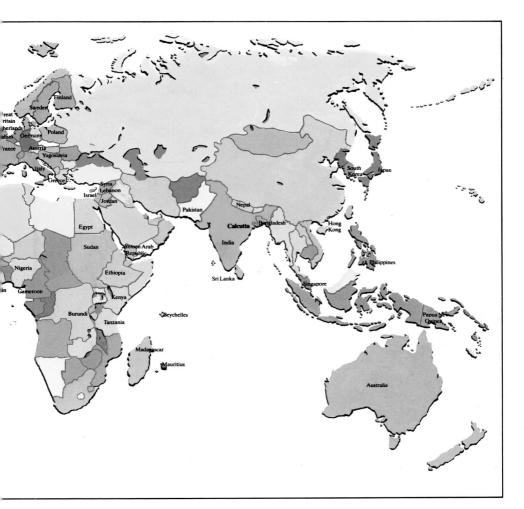

Guyana (1)
Peru (2, 1B)
Uruguay (1)
Venezuela (5)
<u>*Central America & West*</u>
<u>*Indies*</u>
Cuba (1)
Dominican Republic (2, 1B)
El Salvador (1B)
Grenada (1)
Guatemala (1, 3B)
Haiti (4, 1B)
Honduras (2, 1B)
Jamaica (1)
Mexico (4, 1B)
Nicaragua (1)
Panama (2)

Puerto Rico (1)
<u>*Europe*</u>
Austria (1)
Belgium (1)
Finland (1B)
France (2, 1B)
German Democratic Rep. (2)
Germany, Fed. Rep. of (3)
Great Britain (6, 1B)
Greece (1)
Ireland (Eire) (1)
Italy (12, 1B, 1C, 1BC)
Netherlands (1)
Poland (3)
Portugal (2)
Spain (2)
Sweden (1B)

Yugoslavia (2)
<u>*Africa*</u>
Benin (2)
Burundi (2)
Cameroon (1)
Egypt (3)
Ethiopia (6, 1B)
Ghana (1B)
Kenya (2, 1B)
Madagascar (2B)
Mauritius (1, 1B)
Nigeria (1B)
Rwanda (2)
Seychelles (1)
Sudan (2)
Tanzania (3, 1B)
<u>*India (143, 46B, 1C)*</u>

For More Information...

Organizations

The following organizations provide money, food, equipment, and services to hungry, sick, and homeless people around the world. Some of these groups have newsletters or magazines that can give you helpful information about their projects. When you write to them, be sure to tell them exactly what you would like to know, and include in your letter your name, address, and age.

Organizations associated with Mother Teresa's efforts —

Mother Teresa, M. C.
Missionaries of Charity
54A Lower Circular Road
Calcutta   700016
India

Co-Workers Links with Youth
Mr. Tony and Mrs. Lillian Miceli Ferrugia
Villa Elana, Ta X'biex
Malta

Brother Andrew, M. C.
Missionaries of Charity Brothers
7 Mansatala Row
Kidderpore, Calcutta   700023
India

Co-Workers National Link — U.S.A.
Mrs. Vi Collins
5106 Battery Lane
Bethesda, MD 20814

Other concerned groups —

American Friends Service Committee
Finance Division
Africa Hunger and Development
1501 Cherry Street
Philadelphia, PA 19102

Lutheran World Relief
360 Park Avenue
New York, NY 10010

Bread for the World
802 Rhode Island Avenue NE
Washington, D.C. 20018

Oxfam America
115 Broadway
Boston, MA 02116

CARE
660 First Avenue
New York, NY 10016

World Relief
Box WRC
Wheaton, IL 60187

Catholic Relief Services
1011 First Avenue
New York, NY 10022

World Vision
919 W. Huntington Drive
Monrovia, CA 91016

Organizations with special programs for children —

International Child Health Foundation
P.O. Box 1205
Columbia, MD 21044

United Nations Children's
Fund (UNICEF)
United Nations
New York, NY 10017

Save the Children Federation
54 Wilton Road
Westport, CT 06880

SOS Children's Villages
1170 Broadway
New York, NY 10001

Books

The following books will help you learn more about Mother Teresa, her country, her dedication to humanity, and the problems of poverty in the world. Check your local library or bookstore to see if they have them or can order them for you.

About Mother Teresa —

Mother Teresa: A Sister to the Poor. Giff (Viking)
Mother Teresa: Friend of the Friendless. Greene (Childrens Press)
Mother Teresa. Craig (David & Charles)

About India —

Bullock Carts and Motorbikes. Roy (Atheneum)
Getting to Know India. Laschever (Coward/Putnam)
India. Raman (Fideler)
India: An Ancient Land, A New Nation. Sarin (Dillon)
India: Land of Rivers. Bryce (Nelson)
India: Now and Through Time. Galbraith (Houghton Mifflin)
India: Old Land, New Nation. Watson (Garrard)
India: The Challenge of Change. Traub (Messner)
Indian Independence. Ashton (David & Charles)
India's Children. Shorter (Viking)
The Land and People of India. Modak (Lippincott)
Let's Travel in India. Geis (Childrens Press)
Made in India: The Story of India's People. Yaukey (Knopf)
Mother India's Children. Rice (Pantheon)
We Live in India. Sandal (Franklin Watts)
Young India: Children of India at Work and at Play. Norris (Dodd, Mead)

Glossary

Chapatti
Indian unleavened bread, baked on a hot metal plate, and similar in appearance to a flour tortilla.

Co-Workers
About 70,000 people around the world who have pledged to help others. The full name is the Co-Workers of Mother Teresa, International. The group was founded by Ann Blaikie and Josepha Gosselke in 1954 as a spiritual family pledged to support those who are not being reached by social programs in their own society.

Dhal or *daal*
A soup-like dish made of lentils and eaten with rice and curry.

Dowry
Money or goods given to in-laws or an intended spouse as part of a marriage price. In some cultures, the family of the bride offers the dowry. In other cultures, the groom provides it. In India the dowry is now illegal, but common anyway.

Ek Dil
A newsletter Mother Teresa uses to reach members of the now far-flung houses of the Missionaries of Charity. The title means "one heart" in Hindi.

Grotto
A place of rest that resembles a cave, a shrine. It is generally a peaceful quiet place. In modern times, people build grottos as places for meditating.

Hindu
A follower of Hinduism, a religion common in India and dating back to 1500 B.C. Hindus follow the teachings of the Vedas, ancient texts written in Sanskrit. These texts discuss the caste system, reincarnation, and other Hindu beliefs.

Hostel
A place of shelter, an inn. In some countries, hostels are inexpensive places where people with little money can rest when traveling.

Hospice
A place of shelter for the sick or poor. While monks usually ran hospices, now hospitals use hospices for terminally ill patients and their families.

Lepers
A term used by some people to refer to people who have leprosy. More recently these people are called leprosy sufferers, and the disease is called Hansen's

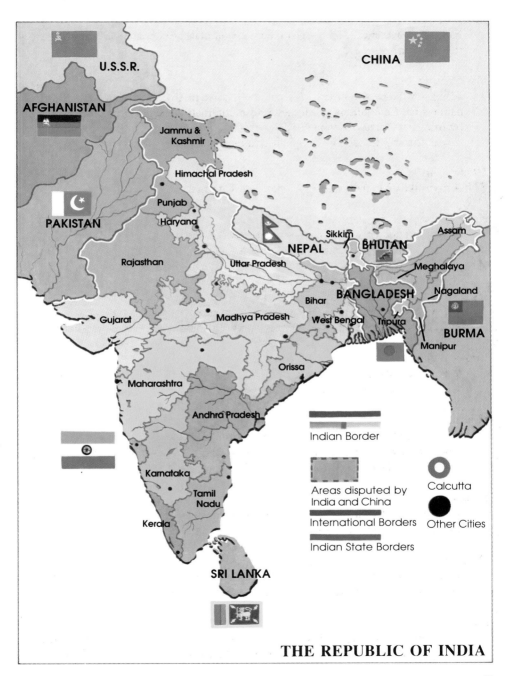

THE REPUBLIC OF INDIA

Disease rather than leprosy. This disease, now curable, affects the nerves and skin and can eat away parts of the body. It appears most often in hot, humid places with unsanitary conditions. Of the 250-300 cases of leprosy reported in the States each year, about ninety-five percent occur in people who emigrated from warmer countries.

Mosque

A Moslem house of prayer, of different sizes and types. The larger Friday mosque must hold all the congregation during Friday prayers. All have three features: a courtyard, a *qibla* wall (one that faces the holy city of Mecca), and a roofed prayer hall. In Islamic societies, mosques are also used as community centers for political and social purposes.

Motherhouse

The original convent of a religious order or the convent in which the Mother Superior of an Order lives. The Motherhouse of the Missionaries of Charity is in Calcutta.

Muslim

A follower of Islam, a religion founded by Mohammed, the Prophet. Muslims follow the teachings of the Koran and the Sunna, which is handed down through a collection called the Hadith. The Koran concerns what God said to Mohammed, and the Hadith concerns what Mohammed said or did in particular situations.

Novice

Someone training to be a sister or brother in a religious order. Also used to refer to a beginner at anything. The period of time a religious person spends as a novice is called the novitiate, as is the place where the novice stays.

Retreat

A period of time people use to think about their lives. Places where people go for the quiet needed to think are called retreats. In religious orders, a retreat usually includes renewing commitment to spiritual life. Mother Teresa's inspiration to form the Missionaries of Charity was the result of a retreat.

Sari

The traditional dress of Hindu women. It is made of about 18 feet of cloth that is three feet wide and wrapped about the body. The Missionaries of Charity each have three *saris* as part of their few possessions.

Sick and Suffering Co-Workers

Over 1300 sick and disabled people who pray for the Missionaries of Charity. It was founded in 1952 by Jacqueline de Decker, who had wanted to join Mother Teresa in 1949 but was too ill to do the work.

Chronology

1910   Agnes Gonxha ("flower bud") Bojaxhiu is born in Skopje, then part of Albania, the youngest of three children.

1919   Agnes' father dies. Agnes' mother builds a needlework and fabric business to support the family. Agnes' brother, Lazar, attends military school and Agnes and her sister, Age, go to a local school.

1928   Agnes goes to Paris and interviews to become a nun in an Irish order, the Sisters of Loreto. She is accepted but must first learn English in Dublin. She then leaves for Calcutta.

1929   **January 6** — Agnes arrives in Calcutta and goes to Darjeeling as novice.
May 23 — She names herself Teresa after a Carmelite nun.

1930   Gandhi and thousands of followers march to the sea in protest of the salt tax imposed by the British government.

1931   **May 24** — Sister Teresa takes her first temporary vows of poverty, chastity, and obedience. She teaches at a Loreto school in Calcutta.

1937   **May 14** — Sister Teresa takes her final vows, in Darjeeling.

1943   Millions die in Bengal because of severe famine.

1946   Muslim-Hindu conflict worsens as Muslims press to separate from Hindu India and set up the nation of Pakistan.
August 16 — Muslim League declares a "Direct Action Day" in Calcutta. Riots result.
September 10 — Sister Teresa receives her "call within a call." She asks to work with Calcutta's poor.

1947   **August 15** — India achieves independence and separates into Hindu India and Muslim Pakistan. Violence erupts and millions leave their homes.

1948   Sister Teresa becomes an Indian citizen.
December — Sister Teresa requests permission from her Mother General to leave the convent and live among the poor.
April 12 — Pope Pius XII gives permission to Sister Teresa to leave the convent, but she does not receive the letter until August.
August 16 — Sister Teresa leaves the convent, wearing a white *sari*, and goes to the Medical Mission Sisters to learn nursing.
December 21 — Sister Teresa works in the slums for the first time.

1949	**March 19** — Sister Agnes joins Teresa as her first helper.
1950	Sister Teresa proposes the Rule for the Society of the Missionaries of Charity. Besides the vows of poverty, chastity, and obedience, members of the Order commit themselves to working for the poor. **October 7** — Pope Pius XII authorizes Sister Teresa's Order. She becomes Mother Teresa.
1952	Mother Teresa opens Kalighat, a shelter for the dying.
1953	**February** — Mother Teresa and twenty-eight sisters move to 54A Lower Circular Road, which becomes the Order's Motherhouse.
1955	The first children's home, Shishu Bhavan, is opened in Calcutta.
1959	**March** — Clinic and refuge for leprosy sufferers opens at Titagarh.
1960	**October 25** — Mother Teresa flies to the United States to deliver talks to and accept donations from the Catholic Relief Services. **November** — Mother Teresa solicits aid in European cities and sees her brother, Lazar, for the first time in thirty years.
1961	Sisters go to Asanol in West Bengal to work with leprosy sufferers.
1962	**September** — Mother Teresa receives India's Padma Sri Award.
1963	**March 25** — First Missionary Brothers of Charity is founded by a former Jesuit, Father Ian Travers-Ball, now Brother Andrew.
1964	**December** — Pope Paul VI visits India and donates a limousine to Mother Teresa. She raffles it.
1965	**February 1** — Pope Paul VI issues the *Decretum Laudis*, which allows the Missionaries of Charity to open houses outside India. **July 26** — First foreign mission opens in Cocorote, Venezuela.
1967	**March** — Missionary Brothers of Charity is accepted by the Catholic Church as an Indian congregation.
1969	Shanti Nagar, "town of peace," opens for leprosy sufferers in West Bengal.
1971	**January 6** — Mother Teresa receives the Pope John XXIII Peace Award. **April** — East Pakistan becomes Bangladesh. War displaces millions who flee to India.

October — Mother Teresa receives the John F. Kennedy International Award for years of service.

1972   **November 15** — Mother Teresa receives the Jawaharlal Nehru Award for International Understanding.

1973   **February** — House opened by Missionary Brothers in Saigon, now Ho Chi Minh City.
April 25 — Mother Teresa receives the Templeton Prize for Progress in Religion in London.

1974   **February** — Missionary Brothers open house in Phnom Penh.

1975   **July** — Brothers open first house in the United States.
October — Mother Teresa receives the Albert Schweitzer International Prize for her work with India's poor.

1976   **November 25** — Mother Teresa speaks to the World Conference on Religion and Peace in Singapore.

1977   **June 10** — Mother Teresa receives honorary degree from the University of Cambridge, England.

1979   In recognition of her work, Mother Teresa receives Balzan International Prize from President Pertini of Italy.
December 8 — Mother Teresa receives Nobel Peace Prize. In this year, she opens thirteen houses in India and thirteen abroad.

1980   **November 1** — Pope John Paul II becomes the first priest Co-Worker.

1981   Mother Teresa celebrates her Golden Jubilee as a nun, fifty years of service to others and to God.

1982   **June 9** — Mother Teresa receives an honorary doctorate of law degree from Harvard University, rescues thirty-seven children in Lebanon, and opens sixteen more houses.

1983   **June 3** — Mother Teresa admitted to hospital with heart problem.
November — Mother Teresa receives England's Order of Merit.
December 3 — Missionaries of Charity help survivors of the poisonous gas leaked by pesticide plant in Bhopal, India. Thousands are affected.

1985   **January** — Mother Teresa goes to Ethiopia to assess the famine. Over three hundred houses exist all over the world.

Index